READER-FRIENDLY WRITING FOR AUTHORS

OLIVIA ATWATER

STARWATCH
PRESS

Copyright © 2023 by Olivia Atwater
https://oliviaatwater.com
All rights reserved.

No part of this book may be reproduced in any form or by any electronic or mechanical means, including information storage and retrieval systems, without written permission from the author, except for the use of brief quotations in a book review.

INTRODUCTION

Before I ever published my first novel, I worked several different jobs. All of them, I maintain, have played a role in my success as an author (though perhaps the job of 'haunted house zombie nurse' has yet to fully manifest in my writing). It is undoubtedly my job as a technical writer, however, that has had the most impact on my writing.

For those who aren't familiar with technical writing, it is the discipline of writing clear instructional material. Technical writing organises information in a logical, intuitive manner so that it can be easily used. Technical writing is often applied to both manuals and general nonfiction writing. And frankly, it is difficult.

If I were to sum up the main tenets of technical writing, they would be as follows:

1. **Assume your reader knows nothing.**
2. **Expect your reader to be distracted.**

3. **Expect your reader to forget things.**
4. **Follow a consistent pattern.**
5. **Avoid ambiguity.**
6. **Repeat yourself often.**
7. **Repeat yourself often.**

All of these tenets can (and should!) be applied to writing fiction—but somehow, when I pick up books on creative writing, I never see such advice. Instead of advice on how to write clear, unambiguous text, in fact, I often find *counterproductive* advice! I see advice like "show, don't tell" and "omit as many words as possible" and "respect your reader, instead of spelling things out for them".

This book is not those books. Instead, I am going to offer you an alternative perspective on writing, based on including as many readers as possible and making sure that you leave no one behind. As such, this is likely to be my single most controversial book. Don't worry, I'm prepared—I've bought some plot armour to hold off the pitchforks.

If you implement the advice in this book, you will find that readers rarely need to reread your sentences in order to understand them. You will find that readers are able to easily pick back up your book and re-immerse themselves in the story, even when they were previously forced to put the book down. You will find that readers are able to follow along with your story even when listening to music, watching Netflix out of the corner of their eye, or doing chores in between chapters. In short, this book will teach you the science of unblocking your reader.

This book will *not* teach you the basics of English grammar. Though I do my best to give examples of grammatical terms when they appear, much of the advice in this book assumes that you can already diagram a simple English sentence. This book will not teach you how to write a compelling plot, nor will it teach you how to write artful, scintillating prose—nor will any of the advice in this book earn you the respect of your authorial peers, many of whom will likely take a red pen to your writing and confidently declare "don't you know you should be showing instead of telling?"

I do believe, however, that the advice in this book will make your readers' lives easier. And that, more than anything else, has always been my goal.

CHAPTER 1

OVERVIEW

This book starts with a few short chapters of important context explaining the reasoning behind all of the techniques to follow. First, I open with a chapter titled **The Word of Saint Strunk**, wherein I explain the origin of several "timeless" rules of creative writing which you have likely heard before, and offer up some extra context for their use. After this history lesson, I discuss the concept of **Reader Bandwidth** and why it's in your best interests as an author to minimise how much of this bandwidth your readers are forced to expend in order to understand your writing. Lastly, I define the statistical limits of the average reader's attention span in **Too Many Numbers**.

After establishing some context, I jump into some actual techniques to conserve reader bandwidth, starting at the narrative level. For the very first technique, I advise you to **Remember the Glass Onion** as a way to remind your readers of previous hints you've left them.

I then move on to paragraph-level techniques, starting with the answer to the seemingly obvious question, **What's in a Paragraph?** After this, I discuss an alteration to a classic rule you've likely already heard, called **Show, then Tell**. Lastly, I ask you to read a bit of dialogue and guess **Who's Speaking?** in order to learn about ambiguous dialogue.

At the sentence level, I start by examining **What's in a Sentence?** Next, I move on to discuss several common sentence-level ambiguities and their solutions, starting with **Why I Love the Oxford Comma**. After this, I walk you through a bit of relevant gameshow trivia involving **The Mat at the Top of the Hill** in order to explain ambiguous prepositional phrases. I take a brief break in order to tell you why **Negatives are Negative**, before finally explaining the trouble with missing or mismatched subjects in a chapter titled **Headless Clauses**.

At the very end of the book, I conclude with a **Last Word** and send you out to steal back your Oxford commas, once and for all.

CHAPTER 2

THE WORD OF SAINT STRUNK

THE EDITOR'S BIBLE.

The creative writing community quotes several rules as gospel, such as:

- "Use the active voice"
- "Use definite, specific, concrete language"
- "Omit needless words"

In fact, these rules originate from a book called *The Elements of Style*, written by William Strunk in 1918 (later edited and expanded by E.B. White).[1] *The Elements of Style* is probably the closest thing that editors have to a holy book. Thankfully, I am an acknowledged heretic who enjoys questioning holy rules.

All joking aside, there are many fantastic rules and explanations in *The Elements of Style*, and I would still call it required reading for any author who wants to improve their grasp of clarity—in fact, given that the book is now in the public domain and therefore available for free on the Internet, writers have few good excuses not to read it. But while Strunk backed up many of his rules with excellent reasoning, a few of them were clearly born of simple preference. Worse by far, some of Strunk's rules have since been stripped of their context and wildly corrupted into forms that he did not originally intend.

In the rest of this book, I will sometimes reiterate rules from *The Elements of Style*, more or less by coincidence—as I have said, several of the rules in the book are helpful, and they happen to coincide with my own style of editing. Other times, I may contradict these rules entirely, either because I disagree with them or else because I'm Canadian (our punctuation sometimes follows British convention rather than American convention). Righteous editors may attempt to find and silence me for this heresy, which is why I live in the Great White North where they will have to walk uphill both ways in the snow in order to get to me.

If you haven't read *The Elements of Style* but are currently feeling inclined to protest on behalf of Saint Strunk, I will firstly assure you once again that his book is still an excellent read, and worthy of a place on every writer's bookshelf. I will secondly leave you to ponder whether you also intend to defend some of Strunk's more quarrelsome and less well-known advice, taken from the very same book.

Hopefully. This once-useful adverb meaning "with hope" has been distorted and is now widely used to mean "I hope" or "it is to be hoped". Such use is not merely wrong, it is silly.

Insightful. The word is a suspicious overstatement for "perceptive". If it is to be used at all, it should be used for instances of remarkably penetrating vision. Usually, it crops up merely to inflate the commonplace.

Like has long been widely misused by the illiterate; lately, it has been taken up by the knowing and the well-informed, who find it catchy, or liberating, and who use it as though they were slumming.

All saints have their blind spots, and though Mr Strunk was probably correct more often than he was incorrect, responsible writers should read his original work for themselves and ponder each rule separately, rather than taking the entire set of rules as ironclad law. Everyone else should be aware, at least, that many of the holy writing rules they've received have an origin and a context, and that the modern author community does not always apply these rules appropriately.

CHAPTER 3
READER BANDWIDTH

AIN'T NO ONE GOT TIME FOR THIS.

Allow me to paint you a picture of one of your readers.

This reader—we'll call her Olivia—is a mother of two children who also works a 9-5 job. Olivia loves reading thrillers, but she isn't often able to set aside several hours of uninterrupted time in order to enjoy them. Instead, she reads one chapter on public transportation on her way to work, reads another chapter on her lunch break, and then sneaks in a few paragraphs that night while waiting for dinner to finish cooking.

Olivia has very limited **reader bandwidth**. It's not her fault; it doesn't make her stupid. It just means that her brain is split in several different directions at any given time, and that means she's often going to lose her train of thought. But Olivia is still a voracious reader! In fact, thriller novels are her one guilty pleasure, and she goes through several thrillers every month. If you're a thriller author, she's probably read through your entire catalogue and even pre-ordered your next book as soon as she reached your last available novel.

Olivia is one of your most valuable readers. So why are you constantly ignoring her?

So much of the creative writing advice I see revolves around the idea that making things unnecessarily hard for your readers is actually about *respecting* them. If the reader can fill in a word on their own, then that word isn't necessary! *Trust* your reader to remember the little plot detail you snuck into your book three chapters ago! Describe a character's facial expression—but don't tell the reader how that character actually feels, because that's lazy and you don't want to talk down to them. In fact, why are you repeating a character's name so many times when you can just use a pronoun for several paragraphs instead?

Olivia's doing her best, guys. She loves your book. But every time she manages to steal five minutes to read a little more of it, she finds herself going back a page to remember who's talking right now, because you haven't used the character's name in several paragraphs. She's rereading sentences because some of them could technically be read two different ways, all while half of her attention is fixed on the toddler down the hall who might have found a permanent marker. Her brain is already working hard, and every time she's forced to reread something, she's jolted out of enjoying the story itself.

I'm not saying you have to assume that *every* reader is Olivia, or even that you have to cater to her in order to write a book. There's a fine literary tradition of upper-class authors writing for a select group of intellectuals with plenty of time on their hands, and you can aim for that tradition. But if you're writing genre fiction and you happen to want Olivia's money, then it certainly pays to make things easier for her.

It's worth noting that there are plenty of Olivia types out there who have their own reasons to struggle with uninterrupted reading. Dyslexic readers, ADHD readers, and readers for whom English is a second or third language are all a part of your potential audience—and if they're having difficulty with your prose because you "respected" them too much, that doesn't make them stupid.

The next time someone asks you to "respect your reader", consider telling them about Olivia. Instead of trusting Olivia to think harder and reread a few paragraphs, it might behoove us all to show her a little more grace.

RAMPS AND STAIRS.

Even your non-Olivia readers will sometimes have bad days where they might appreciate a little less tough love and a little more empathy. We've all fallen sick before and taken medicine which confuses our mental state. I can remember several instances where I found myself laying in bed, feeling useless and frustrated—good for very little other than reading a book or watching a television show. But plot points and dialogue which I might normally have found easy to understand sometimes got garbled because of the Nyquil. Often, I'd need to rewind the show or reread the paragraph several times in order to make my brain process what was going on.

Sometimes, after enough confusion, I'd just give up and crawl back under the covers.

Everyone has bad days, and it's not insulting to make space for that in your writing. I liken this to businesses that have both ramps for people with wheelchairs and stairs for people without them. Sometimes, the people without wheelchairs might be tired or achy enough to need a ramp—or maybe they have a cart full of items which would be difficult to push up the stairs. Either way, having the ramp around is a good idea.

Add ramps to your writing. Maybe your readers who are fortunate enough not to require a wheelchair will complain. But then, people who don't currently require wheelchairs sometimes end up suddenly needing that wheelchair later in life—at which point, they might appreciate the ramp far more.

CHAPTER 4

TOO MANY NUMBERS

7 SHORT-TERM MEMORY SLOTS.

You might be surprised to know that the average person can only hold onto 7 pieces of short-term information at any given time. This statistic is based, furthermore, on the assumption that the person in question is currently devoting their full attention to only one task. Do you remember the last time you tried to memorise a phone number after hearing it only once? Imagine how much more difficult that would be if you were trying to remember both a new name *and* a new phone number, after only one repetition. Now imagine how difficult it would be for you to hold onto this information while also doing your laundry.

Words are slightly easier than phone numbers for people to hold onto, for the obvious reason that phone numbers are arbitrary—the individual numbers in a phone number have no inherent pattern, and therefore cannot be subjected to cognitive shortcuts. For this reason, businesses often turn the last few digits of their phone number into letters that make up an easily memorable word. By connecting these numbers into a word, the person's mind is able to group them as a single coherent concept, turning them into one piece of information rather than several.

These seven short-term memory slots explain a lot about how readers process information and how writers can improve a reader's ability to process their prose. Chapters, paragraphs, and sentences can all be seen as chunks of information which you are trying to group together in ways that the reader's brain will find most easily digestible. The more you relate your building blocks to one another and draw obvious connections between them, the easier your reader will find it to hold onto more of the information in your story at once.

Your goal as an author when writing chapters, paragraphs, and sentences should therefore be to **minimise the reader's short-term memory usage** and **maximise the natural logical flow from one idea into the next idea**. As this book goes on, I'll explain some techniques which you can apply at all levels in order to do this.

CHAPTER 5

REMEMBER THE GLASS ONION

SHERLOCK HOLMES AND THE MISSING BOOT.

Do you remember the missing boot at the very beginning of the story? You might not have realised it at the time, but that missing boot was the crucial clue which identified the murderer! Please, let me walk you through my investigation, step by step...

Anyone who's ever read a murder mystery novel will recognise the paragraph above as part of a parlour scene—a traditional beat at the end of a mystery where the investigator identifies the murderer and explains how the murder was committed. Along the way, the investigator also explains how *they* identified the murderer during the course of their investigation, reminding the reader of clues which they might have missed along the way.

A murder mystery without a parlour scene would generally be considered incomplete. But while most authors and readers would agree that there is value in pointing out physical clues to the reader and connecting them to a conclusion, this advice somehow never crosses the divide into other areas of storytelling, like themes and character conflicts. Instead, as always, I see the advice to "respect your reader" and trust them to remember one crucial line of conversation several chapters prior which might impact the current situation.

Obviously, I am not a proponent of trusting that your reader has a photographic memory for any reason whatsoever. Instead, I apply parlour scene logic to every aspect of the story that I can, dropping brief, extra lines to remind readers of relevant information which they might have since forgotten. For instance, a book with themes about changing the world might have a bit of dialogue like this:

> "I'm just trying to follow the advice that you gave me—" Ella began.
>
> "My advice was wrong!" John blurted out. "You tried to tell me, and I didn't listen. Go back to trying to change the world, Ella. Maybe you can't see it, but it's *working*."

This isn't an awful bit of dialogue, in the context of what we're discussing—it *does* remind the reader that John once gave Ella advice, and then it tells the reader that John now thinks that advice is wrong. But maybe it's been a good long while since the reader actually *read* that chapter, in which case they might have forgotten the advice that John originally gave Ella and why it might be relevant to this scene.

A better version of this dialogue might run as follows:

> "But you told me the world was unfair, and there was nothing I could do about it—" Ella began.
>
> "I was wrong!" John blurted out. "You tried to tell me, and I didn't listen. Go back to trying to change the world, Ella. Maybe you can't see it, but it's *working*."

In this case, Ella has reminded the reader of John's exact advice, in the same way that Mr Holmes might remind Watson about a missing boot from chapter one.

A GLASS ONION AND A PARLOUR SCENE.

The recent murder mystery movie *Glass Onion* had a parlour scene which used this callback technique to explain both the murder *and* the story's central theme—namely, that things are sometimes so obvious that we go searching for a more complicated alternative explanation which doesn't actually exist. Regardless of whether you enjoy the rest of the movie or not, this scene is a fantastic example of how to remind viewers of previous dialogue and motifs which have now become relevant to tying up both the moral of the story *and* the explanation of the murder.

> BENOIT BLANC: I keep returning, in my mind, to the glass onion—something that seems densely layered, mysterious and inscrutable. But in fact, the centre is in plain sight.

Interestingly, *Glass Onion*'s use of this technique has elicited a deeply conflicted audience response. A good portion of the audience seems to have appreciated it—but a minority of the audience *does* feel talked down to, especially if they "saw the glass onion" from the very beginning and therefore didn't require the step-by-step reveal. This division, I think, is the perfect example of the difference between our Olivia readers and our readers with above-average bandwidth to spare. The Olivia viewers *did* require the step-by-step reveal... but some of the viewers who didn't require the reveal thought that the scriptwriters were calling them stupid by assuming they needed the help. It didn't seem to occur to these viewers, somehow, that *someone else* might have required the explanation.

As a rule, I tend to privilege my Olivia readers over the minority of readers who can't tolerate the idea that a book might be throwing a lifeline to someone other than them. But it *is* worth recognising that some readers will take active offence at the techniques in this book, because these techniques are not tailored to their personally preferred reading experience. Alas, you must cater to one type of reader or the other—but you cannot please everyone at once.

CHAPTER 6

WHAT'S IN A PARAGRAPH?

PARAGRAPH TO PARAGRAPH.

How do you actually decide how to group sentences into paragraphs?

Most writers have an instinctive idea of what makes up a paragraph, based on years of reading other people's stories. But this instinctive knowledge can fall short when trying to maximise reader comprehension. Though the act of writing for comprehension can sometimes be inexact, there are still a few considerations you can keep in mind while doing so, listed out below.

- **Write sentences in chronological order.**
- **Write descriptions roughly from top to bottom.**
- **Group sentences into paragraphs by overall concept.**

- **Write all sentences within a paragraph such that the same actor performs all actions in that paragraph (if you can).**
- **When writing dialogue, always start a new paragraph when switching speakers.**
- **Break up large paragraphs before they become too exhausting.**

WRITE SENTENCES IN CHRONOLOGICAL ORDER.

This is the first and most obvious rule of paragraphs: Write things in order. If you find yourself jumping around in the timeline with long tangents about what a character did earlier that morning, you've probably violated this rule and need to reassess your structure as a whole.

Obviously, some books intentionally play with flashbacks and unreliable timelines—but these exceptions to the rule only work well if the *rest* of the book's building blocks are carefully chronological. There's a stark difference between confusing your reader on purpose and confusing them by accident with muddled, disordered prose.

The paragraph below, for example, is chronologically disordered:

> Ella walked into the library. She'd spent the morning at a coffee shop; there were still stains on her shirt where she'd spilled her drink.

Instead of rubber banding your reader back and forth in time, you might approach the paragraph in this way:

> By the time Ella left her morning coffee date, her drink was spilled, her shirt was stained, and her nerves were frayed. She entered the library in a particularly foul mood.

Notice how the earliest events in the day go at the very beginning of the paragraph.

WRITE DESCRIPTIONS ROUGHLY FROM TOP TO BOTTOM.

In the same way that you should describe actions in chronological order, you should also write your descriptions roughly from top to bottom. This is because most readers build mental images step-by-step, first interpreting details explicitly given to them by the text and then filling in the blank spots with their own imagination. Consider the following paragraph:

> Ella had pulled her blonde hair back into a tight long ponytail today. She wore her oldest, most beaten-up boots, and a pair of black sunglasses which had probably gone out of style in the 90's.

The paragraph above is out of order. Once the reader reaches "boots", they've already mentally filled in Ella's face. For many readers, the mention of black sunglasses at the very end will require that they rubber-band their inner eye back up to Ella's face in order to revise it. A revision of this paragraph might look as follows:

Ella had pulled her blonde hair back into a tight long ponytail today. She grimaced against the morning sunlight, hiding behind a pair of black sunglasses which had probably gone out of style in the 90's. The old, beaten-up boots she wore had certainly seen better days—but at least they were sturdy.

If you find that your paragraph becomes bland when reordered, you can try adding more contextual detail, as in the reordered paragraph above.

GROUP SENTENCES INTO PARAGRAPHS BY OVERALL CONCEPT.

Imagine each separate paragraph in your chapter as a book of its own. When the reader starts a paragraph, they "open" a book in their mind and start reading. The first sentence in your paragraph is a kind of book title—it tells the reader what this paragraph-book will be about. Once you've made the implicit promise to talk about this subject in the following paragraph, you have to follow through on it. The more you devolve into tangents or talk about something other than the paragraph-book title in the body of your paragraph, the more you have betrayed your reader's expectations and possibly annoyed them.

For example: Let's say you start a paragraph with the sentence "The library was small and cramped." The reader will expect you to continue expounding on at least one concept within that sentence. You could move on to further describe the library, detailing its bookshelves and furniture. Alternatively, you could elaborate on the claustrophobic feelings your main character has started feeling upon entering the library.

What your reader will *not* expect is something akin to the following.

> The library was small and cramped. Ella glanced at John as they entered, wondering if he was still upset with her.

Though this paragraph is *chronologically* ordered, it is *conceptually* incoherent.

There are two possible solutions to the problem above. The first solution would be to separate the library's description into its own paragraph and elaborate further on that description before moving on to a new paragraph about Ella, John, and their feelings towards one another, as below.

> The library was small and cramped. Tall oak bookshelves stretched to the ceiling, stacked with heavy leather tomes.
>
> Ella glanced at John as they entered the room, wondering if he was still upset with her.

The second solution would be to tie the library's claustrophobic feel to Ella's worries about John, as below.

> The library was small and cramped—or perhaps Ella was imagining that smallness, preoccupied as she was by her recent argument with John. The walls of the room leaned in upon her as she wondered once again whether he was still upset with her.

You might also notice that relating the library's smallness to Ella's emotions makes the entire paragraph feel more unified and easier to follow. This is because the paragraph has explicitly connected the two concepts, essentially turning them into *one* concept, which takes up less short-term memory space.

WRITE ALL SENTENCES WITHIN A PARAGRAPH SUCH THAT THE SAME ACTOR PERFORMS ALL ACTIONS IN THAT PARAGRAPH (IF YOU CAN).

When a reader starts a new paragraph, their brain will generally fixate on the first actor mentioned in that paragraph, and will slot that actor into their first short-term memory slot. Every time someone takes action within the paragraph, the reader *assumes* that the actor in the first slot is the one taking this action until proven otherwise. Below is an example of mismatched actors within a paragraph.

> Ella walked into the library. Striding far ahead of her, John reached the bookcase first.

Because the reader has slotted "Ella" into their first short-term memory slot, they will *begin* to read the words "Striding far ahead" as though Ella is the person doing the striding. Upon reaching the words "far ahead of her", the reader must then switch contexts, re-envisioning the scene with John striding in place of Ella. There are several possible solutions to this problem, one of which is below.

> Ella walked into the library, lagging self-consciously behind John, who reached the bookcase first.

Note how the sentence now describes Ella's positioning from *her* perspective. Instead of John striding, we now have Ella lagging.

WHEN WRITING DIALOGUE, ALWAYS START A NEW PARAGRAPH WHEN SWITCHING SPEAKERS.

This is a fairly simple, well-understood rule. When switching speakers in the middle of a dialogue, you should always start a new paragraph. You need not start each paragraph with the quote itself—sometimes, you may wish to describe the speaker in some way before jumping into the quote, as below.

"Can we talk about what happened earlier?" Ella asked carefully.

John scowled. "I'd rather not," he replied.

(Later, I'll discuss the importance of using proper nouns and dialogue tags with each new speaker in the section **Who's Speaking?**)

BREAK UP LARGE PARAGRAPHS BEFORE THEY BECOME TOO UNWIELDY.

Finally, it pays to remember that large paragraphs exhaust reader bandwidth. As soon as a reader mentally opens your paragraph-book, they instinctively start trying to hold onto all information in the paragraph at once, assuming that it all connects up in a relevant fashion. The longer a paragraph goes on, the more exhausting this becomes, and the less the reader is able to follow new information.

Once a paragraph reaches a certain length, you should start looking for natural places to break it apart into smaller conceptual pieces.

CHAPTER 7

SHOW, THEN TELL

WHY NOT BOTH? BOTH IS GOOD.

> Ella's heart beat quickly. Her throat was tight. Her mouth was dry. Suddenly, she found it difficult to speak.

Half of the people who just read this paragraph are assuming that Ella is scared. Others have decided that she is angry. Still others have decided that she has just fallen head-over-heels in love with someone.

All of them could plausibly be right.

Most of the time, the scene in which this paragraph takes place will have extra context surrounding it. In a scene where Ella has just confronted a monster, "Ella is frightened" is probably the correct analysis. But other times, the context is somewhat less clear than you might think. Many romance novels enjoy the enemies-to-lovers trope, where characters are simultaneously attracted to and repulsed by one another. In a book like this, Ella's physical reactions could mean that she is in love, that she is angry, or that she is *both* at the same time.

In cases such as this, it's often just best to add a few extra words to clarify the situation for the reader, as below.

> Ella's heart beat quickly. Her throat was tight. Her mouth was dry. Suddenly, she was just so utterly furious that she found it difficult to speak.

The version above has clarified what Ella is feeling, so the reader cannot possibly mistake it—but while we are directly *telling* the reader what Ella feels, we have first spent several sentences *showing* what she feels so that the reader can easily picture it in their mind's eye.

First, we show. Then, we tell.

CHEKHOV'S SHOWING.

The Russian playwright Anton Chekhov is most famous for the concept of Chekhov's Gun. But the idea of "show, don't tell" probably originated from another of his quotes, as follows:

> "Don't tell me the moon is shining; show me the glint of light on broken glass."

It's a beautiful line, and it has a lot going for it. There's only one problem: We don't know from the second half of the line if we're looking at sunlight or moonlight. Presumably, Chekhov assumed that the rest of the story's surrounding context would make it clear that it was night time... but how far would one need to read into the paragraph before that *does* become clear?

Imagine, if you would, a reader who has pictured sunlight on broken glass and a furtive conversation happening in the cold light of day, in the middle of a park. Suddenly, the reader hits another "show" line which mentions the darkness outside; now, they blink and return to the very beginning of the scene, rereading everything with a different picture in mind.

The reader's ability to focus on the story has been interrupted. Their enjoyment, too, has been interrupted. In this crucial moment, they might well put down the book and decide to start again later, once they have safely dispelled their initial mistaken image of the scene.

I do hope it goes without saying that you don't want readers putting down your book unless they absolutely must.

Either way, Chekhov's original rule has since been flattened and divorced from its original context. Most writers haven't even heard this advice in its original form. Instead, they've heard the rule "show, don't tell".

Your average American genre reader has never read Anton Chekhov's work—nor would they likely enjoy it. As such, I think it's only fair to suggest that you take both his original advice and its later, corrupted form with at least a pinch of salt. It's not terribly onerous, after all, to both show *and* tell.

CHAPTER 8

WHO'S SPEAKING?

HE SAID, SHE SAID.

A few years ago, I picked up a copy of a friend's book for some relaxing reading. The story was fantastic; the characters were intriguing. But within the first few pages, I had to put down the book to handle some laundry. When I later returned to open it again, I landed on a line of dialogue with no attribution, roughly in the style below.

"But I didn't actually do—"

"You did do."

"You're deliberately misinterpreting."

"*You're* being deliberately forgetful."

"This conversation is over."

I stared at the page for several seconds, utterly unable to remember which character was speaking at any given time. The dialogue was quick and punchy and entertaining... but I had no idea what was going on! I couldn't envision the scene in my head. In the end, I had to flip back to the previous page in order to remind myself which character had started the conversation in the first place so I could then alternate between characters in my head with each successive line. This time, I knew I had to finish the entire chapter in one go, or else I might lose track of whose turn it was to speak again.

Many authors *love* the tagless style above, because they feel it makes for a better conversational flow. But in this particular case, I was the Olivia—and instead of improving the conversational flow for me, this style stopped that flow dead in its tracks. Let me tell you, very little spoils the mood of a scene more than having to reread two pages just to figure out who's actually saying what.

I later told my friend what had happened between my laundry and the end of the chapter, and she took several days to ponder the issue. Eventually, she rewrote the scene to add some conversational tags and told me that it had improved the story quite a bit.

Since this experience, I have made it a rule in my own writing to add a dialogue tag to every quotation, using at least one instance of the speaker's proper name in each separate paragraph. Often, this means that I can't convey breathless, snappy dialogue in quite the same way—but frankly, the laundry was always going to interfere with any snappiness, regardless. A simple rewrite of the dialogue above might therefore look something like this:

"But I didn't actually do—" Ella started.

"You did do," John replied coolly.

Ella narrowed her eyes. "You're deliberately misinterpreting," she accused him.

"*You're* being deliberately forgetful," John shot back.

Ella turned on her heel and stormed for the door. "This conversation is over," she declared.

I know, I know. It's basically artless. Utter pedestrian rubbish.

But Olivia will thank you for it.

WHAT WAS YOUR NAME AGAIN?

I'll pick on a different author friend for a moment (you know who you are, bless you). Their book, too, was instantly engaging. But while this author managed to slip in the main character's name on page one, they then spent *three pages* using only the word "she" to refer to that character.

Halfway through page two, I realised that I had actually forgotten the main character's name. This was a bizarre and embarrassing happenstance, rather like being introduced to a new business associate and forgetting their name in the first five minutes. Had I been asked to tell someone about this character, I would have been forced to hem and haw until halfway through chapter one, when my dear author friend finally rediscovered her main character's name.

This is, again, a particularly egregious example. Most authors do not go several pages without ever mentioning the main character's name, unless they are writing in first-person perspective. But the problem of far-too-many pronouns can rear its head in other ways, as in the paragraph below.

> Ella leapt at Gale, bringing her sword down onto her shoulder. She screamed in fury.

There are a *lot* of pronouns in that paragraph. Normally, it would be safe to assume that any "she" or "her" pronouns will refer to the female subject of the first sentence in the paragraph, aka Ella. But this isn't always the case, especially in combat scenes where people are constantly attacking each other, then dodging, and sometimes yelling.

At least one distracted reader is going to read the paragraph above—and then read it again, and again, just to be absolutely sure they've understood it. This is a lot more effort than any reader wants to spend on a single paragraph, especially in the middle of an otherwise exciting, fast-paced fight scene.

Sometimes, you just need to bite the bullet and use more proper nouns. Yes, even if this requires you to repeat a name twice in the same paragraph.

> Ella leapt at Gale, bringing her sword down onto the other woman's shoulder. Ella screamed in fury.

Obviously, we've now repeated the exact same subject twice in a row, which is generally frowned upon. Because of this, we might rearrange the second sentence, like so.

> Ella leapt at Gale, bringing her sword down onto the other woman's shoulder. A raw scream of fury tore its way from Ella's throat.

Any time you find yourself with two or more people in a scene using the same pronoun, you should go through every instance of that pronoun and make sure it's unambiguous. Don't make your readers perform detective work just to figure out who's doing what at any given time. Forcing your reader to figure things out from context isn't about respecting them—all it does is make their life harder and drag them out of the action.

CHAPTER 9

WHAT'S IN A SENTENCE?

HOW LONG SHOULD A SENTENCE BE?

In pursuit of brevity, which is (I hear) the soul of wit, many authors have advised that your sentences should be as short as humanly possible. These authors are wrong.

Reread the paragraph above. You will notice that the first sentence is much longer than the second sentence. This is part of what keeps the paragraph interesting to read. If I were to break down every clause in the paragraph above until I had the shortest sentences possible, here is how it might read.

> I hear that brevity is the soul of wit. Many authors pursue brevity. They advise that your sentences should be as short as humanly possible. These authors are wrong.

Brevity, I should be clear, is less about how long your sentences are in a literal sense and more about how much space your sentences take up in someone's short-term memory. A sentence which is longer but which is more conceptually complete and which flows in a more natural, logical manner may well take up less reader bandwidth than a series of shorter, more direct sentences. A sentence using "which" in the appropriate places may take up less of your reader's bandwidth, because the reader is able to breeze through the sentence without micro-pausing to replace the missing instances of "which" in their own mind.

But brevity is not the whole of writing, and obviously, it must sometimes give way to style. As such, organising clauses into sentences is both an art and a science. Below, I go into some rules you should consider when trying to form your sentences—but only practice and experience will teach you which rules to prioritise at any given time.

- **Write clauses in chronological order.**
- **Start a new sentence when changing actors.**
- **Group an independent clause with the previous independent clause if the first clause directly causes the second.**
- **Use, at most, three independent clauses before starting a new sentence.**
- **Limit commas, both visible and implied.**

WRITE CLAUSES IN CHRONOLOGICAL ORDER.

As with paragraphs, your sentences should always flow chronologically. Consider the sentence below, which is chronologically disordered:

> Ella walked into the library, having first checked her watch for the time.

This sentence can be fixed as below.

> Ella checked her watch before walking into the library.

A better solution, of course, would be to give the watch-checking more room to breathe in its own paragraph, before moving on to a separate paragraph about walking into the library.

START A NEW SENTENCE WHEN CHANGING ACTORS.

Changing actors requires your reader to recalibrate the subject of a sentence. Your reader's brain will catch on to this recalibration more immediately and with less effort if you clearly separate the two actors into their own sentences, as below.

Ella snorted, and John looked away.

Ella snorted. John looked away.

There are exceptions to this rule, of course. In the above example, for instance, if the writer is aiming to directly *contrast* Ella's casual reaction with John's discomfort, the sentence below will do that nicely.

Ella snorted—but John looked away.

The next rule involving causation may also cause you to violate this rule on a fairly regular basis.

GROUP AN INDEPENDENT CLAUSE WITH THE PREVIOUS INDEPENDENT CLAUSE IF THE FIRST CLAUSE DIRECTLY CAUSES THE SECOND.

An independent clause is a single, self-contained idea which can stand on its own as a complete sentence. Independent clauses may be joined together with conjunctions ("and", "or", "but", etc.), colons, semi-colons, or em dashes, but they should only be joined in this way when the two clauses in question are related to one another. When one independent clause *causes* the next independent clause, as below, you should almost always join the two clauses into the same sentence, rather than leaving them as two separate sentences.

Ella pricked her finger on the needle. She cursed loudly, and went searching for a tissue.

Ella pricked her finger on the needle; she cursed loudly, and went searching for a tissue.

As an aside, the advice to "delete all semi-colons from your work" tends to come and go within the writing community. With regard to this advice, both Saint Strunk and I agree: It's shameful advice, and you should ignore it. The semi-colon is a valid punctuation mark with a long and storied history. It has a specific use—and that use is to join two closely related independent clauses without a conjunction.

USE, AT MOST, THREE INDEPENDENT CLAUSES BEFORE STARTING A NEW SENTENCE.

It is obviously possible to join together so many closely-related clauses that you create a run-on sentence. Most of the time, I try to limit myself to, at most, two independent clauses in a single sentence—but sometimes, a third independent clause seems particularly apt, and so I will cheat and add one more. When I join three independent clauses, however, I make sure that I have used two different methods of joining: for instance, a semi-colon and a conjunction.

> Ella's mind whirled with panic; the world tilted, and she found herself swaying on her feet.

I cannot, off the top of my head, recall a time when I have ever dared to join *four* independent clauses together. But now that I have written this sentence, I am sure that some determined reader will go hunting until they find an example of this in my work.

LIMIT COMMAS, BOTH VISIBLE AND IMPLIED.

Many editors will tell you to limit the number of commas you use in a single sentence—but some editors seem to believe that invisible, implied commas don't count against your limit.

Though the sight of too many commas *will* intimidate your reader, this is not the only problem which results from too many commas. Most of the time, a comma represents a verbal pause. Other times, commas do not cause a verbal pause, but are still used to signal a significant change in the conceptual flow of the sentence. Too many conceptual redirections in one sentence are a drain on your reader's bandwidth, regardless of whether you can technically get away with omitting the commas that normally accompany them.

As such, I find it best to keep many of the commas which other editors find technically unnecessary—that way, I can always tell when I've redirected my conceptual flow one too many times. I do not, by any means, keep *all* of the commas which I could technically omit, but I know that my prose has more commas than most other writers generally prefer.

How many commas is too many commas? I will admit, I find the answer to that question to be impossibly personal to each individual writer. This rule, more than any other rule, will require you to experiment in order to find your ideal range of comfort.

CHAPTER 10

WHY I LOVE THE OXFORD COMMA

THE STRIPPERS, JFK, AND STALIN.

Syntactic ambiguity is a fancy phrase for a very simple concept. When you write a sentence which can plausibly be read to mean two or more different things, that sentence is syntactically ambiguous.

There are more ways than one to write a syntactically ambiguous sentence, and this book goes into several different examples. But in this particular chapter, I'm going to focus on the most obvious example of syntactic ambiguity in the English language, and how we normally deal with it.

Consider the following two sentences, recently passed around in an online meme:

"We invited the strippers, JFK and Stalin."

> "We invited the strippers, JFK, and Stalin."

In the first example, which does not use an Oxford comma, there is syntactic ambiguity. Has the author invited two strippers named JFK and Stalin, or have they invited several strippers as well as two deceased world leaders?

The second example is syntactically clear. We know for a fact that the author invited several strippers and two world leaders (though the strippers probably declined, and the world leaders are both dead and therefore unlikely to attend).

The reason the first example is syntactically unclear is because the only comma in the sentence could be read *either* as an appositional comma, which sets off extra information about a noun, *or* as a series comma, which sets off items in a series. (The previous sentence includes some appositional commas, in case the concept confuses you!) By adding a last series comma, also called an Oxford comma, we make it clear that all commas involved are meant to set off items in a series.

The Oxford comma does not solve all possible woes regarding items in a series—and often, you can achieve even better clarity by restructuring the series items instead. For instance, I could rewrite the sentence above as follows:

> "We invited Stalin, JFK and the strippers."

This sentence is syntactically clear, because there is no possible interpretation of it which could use an appositional comma. But maybe there are other sentences in my book which cannot be reordered like this, which therefore *require* the Oxford comma. If I use the Oxford comma only where strictly necessary, I will have some sentences with an Oxford comma and other sentences without it. This inconsistency is jarring to the average reader, and likely to give them pause.

Oxford commas are always safe to use—they never create *more* ambiguity—and so I've learned to love them like the grammatical staple they are.

Now, I suspect that most creative writers already lean towards using Oxford commas in their writing; most of the pushback I've seen against Oxford commas happens with journalists who love their Associated Press style. (Technically, my copyeditor at Orbit also stole my Oxford commas, but I told her I would forgive her because she was very nice about it.) The main reason I've started the section on sentences with this example, however, is because it's a readily understandable example of sentence-level syntactic ambiguity with an easy and obvious solution.

It may take some time for you to get your head around the rest of the examples in this book. But Oxford commas, much like Rick Astley, will never let you down.

CHAPTER 11

THE MAT AT THE TOP OF THE HILL

CHEEKY GAMESHOW LOOPHOLES.

Recently, while avoiding all of my worldly responsibilities, I binged several seasons of a British gameshow called Taskmaster, where five comedians are given a piece of paper with a silly task written on it and asked to complete the task as efficiently and creatively as possible.

In the second series of the show, the contestants are given a task which is written as follows:

> "Place these three exercise balls on the yoga mat at the top of that hill. The task is complete when all three balls sit fully inflated and stationary on the mat. Fastest wins."

This task was clearly meant to be Sisyphean—the exercise balls were far too large for a single person to carry all three at once, and the hill in question was steep and windy. As a result, the show pieced together several clips of comedians chasing giant exercise balls down the hill, yelling lurid curse words as they went.

One comedian, however, hit upon a telling grammatical loophole. Instead of trying to carry the exercise balls up the hill, he strolled up the hill to grab the yoga mat and brought it back down to lay it next to the exercise balls. He then placed all three exercise balls on top of the mat and called the task complete.

When the other comedians discovered this grammatical trick, there was much protesting and gnashing of teeth. But the gameshow host carefully reread the task, and then sent it off to a grammatical nitpicker for consultation. The returned verdict came down in favour of the comedian who had dragged the yoga mat down from the hill—the key sentence of the task could be plausibly read in two different ways, and he had chosen the interpretation which made the task far easier.

I found this syntactic lapse particularly interesting, specifically because the writer of this task had gone out of their way to avoid a purely logical loophole by noting that the exercise balls had to be fully inflated (otherwise, at least one comedian surely would have deflated the exercise balls and carried them up the hill in that state). The fact that the task writer had missed the *grammatical* loophole implied that this syntactic ambiguity was so natural to the English language as to seem nearly invisible to most readers, but glaringly obvious to a few select others.

So what is it that causes the ambiguity in these instructions?

There are two separate prepositional phrases in the first sentence. The order of these prepositional phrases deeply matters to the sentence's interpretation. Consider the following:

"Place these three exercise balls on the yoga mat at the top of that hill."

"Place these three exercise balls on top of that hill on the yoga mat."

The prepositional phrase which immediately follows "exercise balls" ("on the yoga mat") can only be read as modifying the exercise balls. The second prepositional phrase ("at the top of that hill") can be interpreted to modify *either* the exercise balls *or* the yoga mat. Because of this, the first sentence allows an interpretation whereby the contestant can retrieve "the yoga mat at the top of that hill" and then place the exercise balls "on the yoga mat".

Switching the order of these two prepositional phrases can eliminate the ambiguity in this instance—but it's possible to end up in a circumstance where switching the order of your prepositional phrases *won't* eliminate ambiguity. And sometimes, quite honestly, the sentence just sounds awkward that way.

And this is why sometimes, you absolutely require a few extra words in that sentence. Consider:

> "Place these three exercise balls on the yoga mat while it is at the top of that hill."

> "Place these three exercise balls on the yoga mat which is at the top of that hill."

The first sentence clarifies that the yoga mat must be on top of the hill *while* the balls are placed upon it. The second sentence clarifies the alternative interpretation, which implies that the yoga mat may safely be moved.

I think we can all agree that the original syntax of the task made for far better television. But as a writer of fiction, you probably don't want to send your readers *or* your characters chasing after exercise balls over and over, for lack of a single extra 'which'.

"OMIT NEEDLESS WORDS".

You have probably heard the advice "omit needless words" at least once within the creative writing community, whether someone said those exact words to you or else paraphrased them into something like "drop the weasel words" or "shorter is always better". This bit of advice originates from *The Elements of Style*, which I mentioned earlier in **The Word of Saint Strunk**.

Strunk's rule about omitting needless words has been divorced from the other rules which once tempered and accompanied it. As such, many well-meaning writers with only the most basic grasp of technical grammar have applied it in ways it should *not* be applied—for instance, by advising other writers to "delete all instances of 'that' from your manuscript!" or to "use more pronouns and fewer proper nouns!" (More on that particular folly in the previous section, **Who's Speaking?**)

These writers do not actually know which words are "needless", and following their advice will likely turn your prose into a grammatical mess. The gameshow task above is a perfect example of someone eliminating what they *believed* to be a needless word—likely because the writer had it drilled into their head that the word "which" is always superfluous.

In fact, Strunk himself used several instances of "that" and "which" in *The Elements of Style*, and he comments only that "it would be a convenience to all if these two pronouns were used with precision". In the revised edition, E.B. White clearly specifies in a later chapter that these words are not always needless words, as in the quote below.

> But in many cases, the *that* is needed. "He felt that his big nose, which was sunburned, made him look ridiculous." Omit the *that* and you have "He felt his big nose..."

As with the Oxford comma, my advice on the matter is simple: If you do not consider yourself to be an accomplished technical writer, then you are probably not equipped to instinctively recognise when a "that" or a "which" is truly necessary to the syntactic clarity of a sentence. In this case, you have only two real options: Either you must dedicate yourself to learning technical grammar, or else you must ignore your confused contemporaries and sprinkle in far more "that"s and "which"es than the creative writing police would probably find appropriate, in order to safely cover your bases.

CHAPTER 12

NEGATIVES ARE NEGATIVE

DON'T USE NEGATIVES. REPHRASE NEGATIVES.

When readers are distracted or reading very quickly, they can easily overlook a "not" or a "don't" at first glance. Because of this, it's always better to rephrase negatives. Rather than saying what you *don't* mean, say what you *do* mean. For instance:

Ella didn't know what John wanted.

Ella found John's manner confusing.

This is a relatively simple rule, but it can easily sneak up on you, which is why I generally dedicate an entire edit pass to searching for negatives which I think I can safely rephrase.

CHAPTER 13

HEADLESS CLAUSES

STRANGE SUBJECTS.

One of the most common problems I see in prose happens when an author knits two sentences together without first examining whether those sentences share the same subject or not. If the author removes the subject of the second sentence in order to perform this surgery, they create what is known as a null-subject clause or a clause with an implied subject. Personally, I like to call these **headless clauses**, because they inspire such knee-jerk horror in me. For instance, the author might start with the two sentences below.

Ella's eyes narrowed. She knew that John was lying.

But because the author is in a hurry, they make a mistake splicing the two sentences together and end up with *this* sentence.

Ella's eyes narrowed, knowing that John was lying.

Obviously, Ella's eyes cannot "know" anything. The sentence has become garbled—but you'd be surprised how often authors overlook a mistake this egregious and send it straight to print. The proper way to join these two sentences, of course, is to change the subject of the first sentence to "Ella" and then attach the second clause.

Ella narrowed her eyes, knowing that John was lying.

Because it's so very easy to flub this up, I never write headless clauses until I've already written out both sentences separately and made certain that their subjects already agree. In fact, I've found that I write fewer headless clauses in general these days. Sometimes, they're just what the situation requires—but more often, I end up with something closer to the following.

Ella narrowed her eyes. She *knew* John was lying.

I find the above solution to be a little less breathless and a little more punchy. But just so I'm clear, there's nothing inherently *wrong* with headless clauses—as long as you've made certain that the clause's implied subject agrees with the subject of the sentence to which it's attached.

CHAPTER 14

LAST WORD

I know that many authors prioritise action, poetry, or punchiness over clarity. I also know that my own prose could at times be called too clear and not artful enough. But after several years of hearing that neurodivergent people find my books easier to read, I've made a conscious, informed choice to privilege their needs above other possible priorities—and overall, I'm quite content with that decision, whatever its consequences.

You needn't apply all of the advice in this book to your prose every single time, even if you decide that clear and unambiguous writing is one of your major goals; even using just a few of these rules *some* of the time will still improve your overall clarity. At the end of the day, I only hope that the people who read this book will start thinking harder about some of the writing advice they've been given and might sometimes put it to the question. And maybe, occasionally, more writers will consider rewriting a phrase in order to make things easier on the Olivias among their readers.

CHAPTER 15

READER-FRIENDLY EDITING CHECKLIST

NARRATIVE-LEVEL EDITING

- Remember the Glass Onion.

PARAGRAPH-LEVEL EDITING

- Write sentences in chronological order.
- Write descriptions roughly from top to bottom.
- Group sentences into paragraphs by overall concept.
- Write all sentences within a paragraph such that the same actor performs all actions in that paragraph (if you can).
- When writing dialogue, always start a new paragraph when switching speakers.
- Break up large paragraphs before they become too exhausting.
- Show, then tell.

- Always use dialogue tags and identify the current speaker.
- Use proper names at the beginning of paragraphs, as well as when necessary to disambiguate between two characters with the same pronoun.

SENTENCE-LEVEL EDITING

- Write clauses in chronological order.
- Start a new sentence when changing actors.
- Group an independent clause with the previous independent clause if the first clause directly causes the second.
- Use, at most, three independent clauses before starting a new sentence.
- Limit commas, both visible and implied.
- Always use an Oxford comma to set off the last item in a series.
- Clarify ambiguous prepositional phrases with extra words to define their meaning.
- Rephrase negatives.
- Rephrase headless clauses, or double-check that headless clauses use the same implied subject as the sentence to which they are attached.

NOTES

2. THE WORD OF SAINT STRUNK

1. Strunk, William I. 1999. *The Elements of Style*. 4th ed. Upper Saddle River, NJ: Pearson.

ABOUT THE AUTHOR

Olivia Atwater writes whimsical historical fantasy with a hint of satire. She lives in Montreal, Quebec with her fantastic, prose-inspiring husband and her two cats. When she told her second-grade history teacher that she wanted to work with history someday, she is fairly certain this isn't what either party had in mind. She has been, at various times, a historical re-enactor, a professional witch at a metaphysical supply store, a web developer, and a vending machine repairperson.

I send out writing updates and neat historical facts in the Atwater Scandal Sheets. Subscribers also get early access to chapters from each book, before anyone else!

https://oliviaatwater.com
info@oliviaatwater.com

ALSO BY OLIVIA ATWATER

REGENCY FAERIE TALES

Half a Soul

Ten Thousand Stitches

Longshadow

TALES OF THE IRON ROSE

Echoes of the Imperium (Forthcoming — 2023)

ATWATER'S TOOLS FOR AUTHORS

Better Blurb Writing for Authors

Reader-Friendly Writing for Authors